WHY DO I FEEL SO WORRIED?

A KID'S GUIDE TO COPING WITH BIG EMOTIONS

Follow the Arrows
from Anxiety
to Calm ··············>

TAMMI KIRKNESS

THE EXPERIMENT

NEW YORK

THIS BOOK IS DEDICATED
to all the kids with worries on their minds. The
big thinkers, the creative beings, the switched-on kids,
the sensitive souls, the nurturers, the frustrated inventors,
and those who see the world in a different way. From my
heart to yours, I'm sending you calm, deep breaths and a
lightness to layer into your days.

For all the moms, dads, and caregivers of these sensitive,
brave souls: You've got this. Even on the tantrummy days,
the teary mornings, the upset evenings—you've got this.
Your little somebody selected you as the best possible
person to help guide and nurture them through
their life, and that means something.

Contents

Tammi's story

When I was a kid, I tried really hard to make no mistakes. I often compared myself to other kids I knew. I left my homework to the last minute, and I was really hard on myself if I didn't do something perfectly. Overall, I was a bit of a worrier.

When I grew up, I realized that other kids and adults sometimes worried as much as I did, and that was a huge relief. To try to learn more about how our minds work, I read everything I could about why this happens to some people but not so much to others. I studied psychology, became a yoga teacher, learned from monks, and went on to help kids with learning difficulties who often also had trouble with worries.

I wrote this book to teach kids how to cope with worry and be their healthiest, happiest selves. I hope it helps you!

Your friend,
Tammi

Oh, hi there!

Let's get started . . .

Sometimes it's tricky being a kid. There are so many things to learn, and new feelings seem to keep popping up. Sometimes other kids' lives look as if they're easier than ours, and that can feel upsetting.

When big feelings come up, they can be hard to deal with, and when we are worrying on our own, we can feel lonely and scared.

When we worry, it's as if we give away some of our happiness. It can help if we understand why a worry is happening because then we can do something about it.

You are a beautiful, clever kid, and it's important you remember that.

To try to understand all the things going on in your mind, we're going to follow the arrows.

FOR PARENTS & CAREGIVERS

Anxiety can affect anyone at any age. It's tempting to want to protect kids from things that make them worry. However, we know that the more we can help them feel their fears and still do the things they want and need to, the more resilient they will be. When we talk about fear and worry with kids, it can help to destigmatize and normalize the feelings.

The messages in this book draw on yoga and breathing techniques, psychological approaches, life coaching practices, clinical processes, and my own experiences as a young overthinker. We don't choose whether or not to be anxious, but we can choose how to manage the feeling when it arises. Working through these feelings can help us to grow, build flexibility, and foster courage. If at any point your child needs individualized support, please reach out to a relevant qualified support partner such as a counselor, psychologist, or therapist.

Helping someone through emotionally sticky times can act as a mirror for how you cope with that issue too. As you work through this book and the emotional management journey with your young person, it may bring some of your own anxieties to the surface. If this happens, that's okay. It's an opportunity for you to heal things that may have been buried for a while. The more you learn to manage your own mental well-being, the more you will have in your toolkit to be a safe place to land for others.

Remember, kids are incredible. The more we empower them to acknowledge their feelings and provide a safe space to process them, the happier they are.

Using this book with your kid

This book is full of interactive questions for you to read with, or to, your child depending on their age. As you read, gently encourage your child to respond. When there are activity prompts, such as deep breathing, I encourage you to do them along with your child. Whenever possible, in between readings of the book, positively reinforce any efforts they make to use the techniques they've learned.

On many pages, you'll find notes to parents and caregivers—these are to help you understand the context behind particular questions and why certain techniques are being used. Depending on your child's age, you may or may not choose to read these out loud.

When activities prompt kids to repeat something out loud, break it up into short chunks so they can easily repeat it back.

If your child shows signs of being less stressed, such as having a brighter face, looser body language, slowed breathing, or other indications of relaxing, ask them if they are feeling better. If they are, ask them if they would like to finish the book now, and if they would, gently turn to page 127 to check in again before finishing up.

PART ONE

How do I feel?

Feelings are beautiful things.
They send us messages about how
we're reacting to the world around us.
To get started, let's check how
you're feeling right now.

Right now,
WHICH FACE
describes how
you are
FEELING?

WE'LL CHECK IN WITH THESE
AGAIN AT THE END.

SAD   ANGRY   SILLY   HAPPY

FRUSTRATED   SHY   SCARED   EXCITED

WORRIED   LONELY   LEFT OUT   OVERWHELMED

TIRED   SICK   EMBARRASSED   CALM

*NOTE TO PARENTS: *Being able to identify which emotion is present can sometimes bring instant relief to an overwhelmed individual.*

On a scale from 1 to 10, how **STRONG** are those **FEELINGS?**

1   2   3

4   5   6   7

8   9   10

*NOTE TO PARENTS: Knowing the intensity of the worry allows both parent and child to more clearly understand the current moment's severity. Additionally, tracking intensity (we will check in with this scale at the end of the book) can give clues about what brings relief.

PART TWO

Feeling my feelings

Sometimes we feel great and sometimes not so great, but all feelings are important. The more we understand them, the easier things are to cope with. Now, we're going to check in with the most common reasons for our feelings.

Do you have any of these things happening right now?

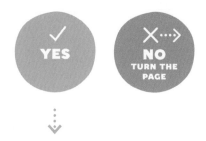

Think about that area
of your body.

Take a big breath
into that area.

With a big breath out,
breathe out the worry.

Repeat twice more.

*NOTE TO PARENTS: *Deep breaths bring extra oxygen to the brain,
allowing the body to relax. Physical sensations are like messengers—
they are there to tell us something is going on that might need our
attention, or let us know we've surpassed our processing capacity.*

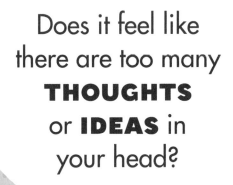

Does it feel like
there are too many
THOUGHTS
or **IDEAS** in
your head?

Stand up.

Bend over like you're going
to touch your toes.

Hold on to each elbow and
dangle forward like a rag doll.

Picture all the unhelpful
thoughts falling out of the top
of your head.

After you count to twenty,
gently stand back up.

Is your
body feeling
STUCK,
like you can't
MOVE it?

Wiggle one of your fingers.

Wiggle a second finger.

Try to wiggle your nose.

Shrug your shoulders.

Shake one leg.

Shake your other leg.

Are you ready for the big shaking finale?

Stand up and shake your whole body out!

*NOTE TO PARENTS: *When we feel anxious, our body often tenses up. Because our mind and body are so closely linked, when we physically shake our body out, it can act as a quick, in-the-moment reset.*

YES

NO
TURN THE PAGE

We're going to try and
worry as hard as we can.

Have a parent (or another
grown-up) set a timer for three
minutes. During this time, you can
worry as much as possible.
When the timer finishes,
it's time to stop worrying.

Before you start, choose one of these
ways to get all your worries out. You can:

List them
out loud

Whisper
them into your
toy's ear

Write
them
down

Draw
them in
a picture

Now, start the timer and start worrying.

After the timer ends, take a big breath
in and then a big breath out.

*NOTE TO PARENTS: *When we keep thinking about the same thing,
it is referred to as rumination. Rumination involves focusing
on a previous negative experience and feeling unable to move on.*

BONUS: *It's not essential, but if you think it might help, you could brainstorm some potential solutions to the worries you listed on a sheet of paper.*

Do you feel **STUCK**? Like you want to **YELL**? Or like you want to **RUN** away?

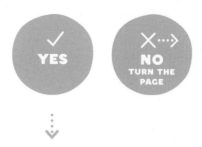

It sounds like you've just had a big shock.
When something frightens us, we often act just like animals do.

When animals are scared, they either freeze completely still,
or get ready to fight or run away quickly.

To help your body return to a feeling of safety, go and get
a cup of water.

Pour a mouthful of water into your mouth and gargle it.
(If you can't gargle or you don't have any water, just take
a breath in through your nose and out through your mouth and
then sing a short song like "Happy Birthday.")

*NOTE TO PARENTS: *Gargling and singing both stimulate our largest cranial nerve (called the vagus nerve) to initiate a feeling of calm. It does this by activating the parasympathetic nervous system, which is responsible for moving the body out of the "fight, flight, or freeze" response into the "rest and digest" relaxation response.*

Is something making you feel **NERVOUS**?

Close your eyes (if that feels okay).

Imagine your nervousness is floating
in the air in front of you.

What color is it?

What shape is it?

What texture is it?

Notice how it's outside of you. Using big breaths,
blow this shape away and up into the sky.

Shrug your shoulders and feel a sense of release.

Do you feel like you have **TOO MUCH** energy and could **BOUNCE** off the walls?

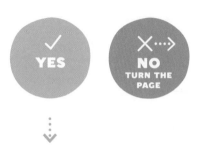

Switch off all gadgets, including phones, tablets, games, computers, and the TV. Turn off or dim all overhead lights.

Is it bedtime?

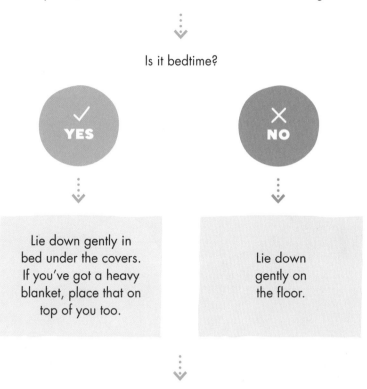

Lie down gently in bed under the covers. If you've got a heavy blanket, place that on top of you too.

Lie down gently on the floor.

Place your hands on your belly. As you slowly breathe in and out, notice how your belly goes up and down under your hands. Do this five times.

Have you
been **MEAN**
to yourself?

Just as it's important to be kind to our friends, it's important to be kind to ourselves.

Let's remember some of the wonderful things about you.

List three things you like about yourself. For example, you have a clever brain, are a good friend, and can tell funny jokes.

Repeat out loud,
"I choose to speak kindly to myself for the rest of the day."

Breathe in deeply. Breathe out all meanness.

YES

NO
TURN THE
PAGE

Do your best to sit
or stand still.

Close your eyes.

Picture long tree roots coming out
of your feet down into the earth.

Imagine how peaceful it is
down there.

Breathe up some of that peace into
your feet and body.

Open your eyes.

Are you
feeling
FIDGETY?

YES **NO**
TURN THE
PAGE

Lie on your back
and place a closed
book on your tummy.

As you breathe in,
notice how the
book rises.

As you breathe out,
notice how the
book lowers.

Do this five times.

Gently stand up.

Can you roll your tongue?

Roll your tongue.	Pretend you are a fan and gently blow air on your left arm, moving your head side to side as you do it.
Breathe in and out three times.	
Do you notice that the air seems cooler as you breathe it in this way?	Now, gently blow air on your right arm in the same way.

*NOTE TO PARENTS: *This is a breathing technique from the yogic tradition that helps you cool down both physically and emotionally. Roughly three to four out of five people can roll their tongue—if it doesn't come naturally to your child, don't force it.*

PART THREE

Figuring out where the worry started

When we understand where our worry started, it can often help. Let's try figuring it out.

Are you
feeling
WORRIED
about . . .

→
School
TURN TO PAGE 44

→
People
TURN TO PAGE 64

→
Home
TURN TO PAGE 92

→
Something else
TURN TO PAGE 104

If you are worried about more than one thing, pick the worry that feels strongest and start there.

Coping in the classroom or at recess can be tricky. If you're feeling worried about something to do with school . . .

TURN THE PAGE →

Are you
having trouble
CONCENTRATING?

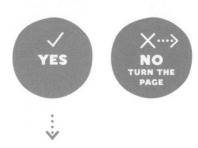

Bring your thoughts to the present moment
by finishing these sentences:

Right now, I can see . . .

I can hear . . .

I can smell . . .

I can taste . . .

I can feel . . .

*NOTE TO PARENTS: *Mindfulness tools like this bring attention into the
present moment, making it far easier to concentrate.*

Have you done something **OVER** and **OVER** again trying to make it **PERFECT**?

Remember, no matter what you create,
you are still a great kid.

If you mess something up and it doesn't look like
you wanted it to, everything will be okay.

Now, take a guess how long it might take you to
finish your task—such as until lunch or dinnertime.

Work on your task until that time rolls around.
Then, wherever you're up to is where you stop.

Remember, finishing something is better than having
something half done because you spent too long
trying to make it perfect.

*NOTE TO PARENTS: *When we try to make things perfect, it leads us
into the trap of black-and-white thinking. Thinking things are either
all good or all bad creates an unhelpful level of pressure. And having the
mindset that someone is either strong or weak, or smart or dumb, leaves
little space to be calm. In reality, we're all a mix of different qualities.*

Are you **LEAVING** something until the **LAST MINUTE**?

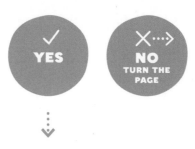

Say out loud what the thing is that you need to do.

Say out loud when you need to do it by.

Say out loud all the reasons you've been putting it off.

Come up with a way to deal with each of those reasons.

Can you do the thing right now?

Start it right away.

Choose a time when you can start it and ask someone to remind you to begin it then.

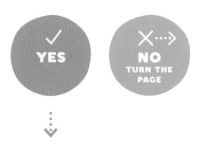

Say out loud what you need help with.

Think about who might have the skills to help you.

Do you know this person?

Go and ask them
for help.

Imagine what ideas this
person would have.

EXTRA NOTE: *Remember that asking for help shows bravery and strength.*

Have you **GIVEN UP** on something before really trying?

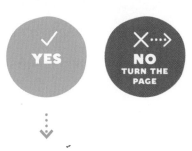

Say out loud the activity you are avoiding. For example, you might need to write a story for school.

Let's break down the task into smaller steps.

Get out a piece of paper.

Together with your parent or grown-up, write down all the steps you need to take to finish this task. With the story example, you might write down that you need to come up with a title, write the first sentence, write five more sentences, read it back to yourself, then hand it in to your teacher.

Put the steps in number order.

Decide when you will start step number one.

*NOTE TO PARENTS: *Kids will often say an activity is "boring" if they feel overwhelmed or out of their depth. If you hear this, ask which part is the trickiest for them and if they'd like some help.*

Have you been **FOCUSING ON** the **PROBLEMS** with something you **MADE**?

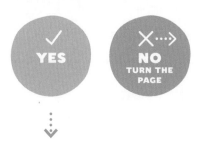

Remember, there is no one "right"
way of doing things.

List out loud three things that you
enjoyed while you were working on this.

List one thing that you like about
your creation.

Breathe in deeply. Breathe out all
feelings of trying to be perfect.

*NOTE TO PARENTS: *Emphasizing the enjoyment of the creative process
is vital to releasing the black-and-white thinking behind perfectionism.*

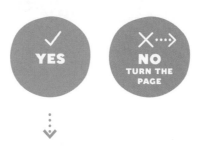

That can't feel nice.
Take a big breath in and a big breath out.

Say out loud what feels like the end of the world. For example,
"If I don't get a good grade, I'll be a terrible student."

Does that thought feel helpful?

On a scale from 1 to 10 (10 being highest), how likely is
that thought to be true?

Let's try looking at that thought another way. For example,
*This is just one of many tests, and my teacher has told me
she loves having me in her class as her student.*

*NOTE TO PARENTS: *This issue is referred to as "catastrophizing."
Catastrophizing assumes the worst-case scenario and can often start small,
then quickly snowball into end-of-the-world-type language and overwhelm.
The earlier these thoughts can be challenged, the better.*

Being able to think differently from others is a great gift, even if it doesn't always feel like that.

What are some of the good things that make your brain different? List two or three. For example, you can play music, draw cartoons, or imagine different worlds.

Say out loud, "I love my mind and my mind loves me. I choose to take care of it and be proud of how it works."

*NOTE TO PARENTS: *There are all sorts of reasons that people might stand out mind-wise. Lots of the world's best thinkers and creators see the world from a different perspective. Remember to encourage the unique gifts that your child has and appreciate how they see the world.*

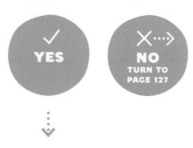

Choose which part of your life is still on your mind:

People

While our friends and family are often our favorite people, sometimes how we feel about them can get wobbly. If you're feeling worried about the people you know . . .

TURN THE PAGE $\rightarrow$

Are you feeling
DISAPPOINTED
or **LET DOWN**
by someone?

Is it fair to expect that person to have done
or said what you wanted?

If possible, go and
talk to this person
about your feelings.
If they aren't around
right now, choose a
time to talk to them.

Remember that
no one is perfect.
Notice where in
your body the
disappointed feeling
is and then let it float
up and away.

Breathe in deeply. Breathe out all tightness
from your body.

Are you really sure that you have upset them?

It's time to say sorry. To get ready to give a really great apology, say these things out loud right now:

- What you did that was hurtful.

- A guess at how the person might be feeling.

- How you're going to stop it from happening again.

Go to the person and say sorry, mentioning all the things you just listed out loud.

Perhaps they aren't upset.

To double-check, you can go and ask them if you hurt them. If they say yes . . .

Are you **PRETENDING** to like something to make someone else happy or to look **COOL**?

Would you still act this way or like this thing if no one else did?

Even though you enjoy acting this way, remember you can stop if it no longer makes you feel happy in the future.

While it might feel easier to fit in if you like the things other people like, in the end, it's best to be yourself. It's time to finish pretending and make more time for being yourself and enjoying the things you really like!

Breathe in deeply. Breathe out any pressure.

Keep being you and remember to always treasure your own opinions.

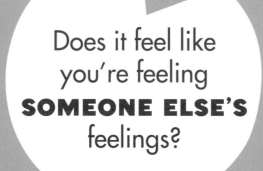

Does it feel like you're feeling **SOMEONE ELSE'S** feelings?

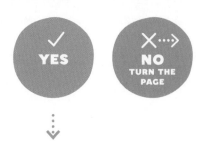

Repeat out loud, "Even though I care a lot about others, it's not my job to feel other people's feelings. I choose now to breathe out all feelings that aren't mine."

Take a big, deep breath in. Breathe out everyone else's worries and feelings.

*NOTE TO PARENTS: *Kids who are particularly empathetic can automatically feel the feelings of others. Once this increased emotional sensitivity is acknowledged and managed, it can be a gift later in life. However, it can often cause emotional fatigue in the short term and is worth keeping an eye on.*

Does it **BOTHER YOU** that one of your friends or siblings might be **BETTER AT SOMETHING** than you?

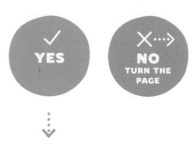

Everyone has their own talents, and
it is very clever of you to see them
in someone else.

Say out loud one thing you can learn from
the other person's talent.

Even if it feels tricky, take a moment
to think about how happy you are that they
have such a great skill.

BONUS:
You could go
and tell them how
good they are at
that particular
thing.

Sometimes our brains feel like they freeze a little during the times when we want to speak. Say out loud what you wished you'd said at the time. Do you still want to say this thing to the person?

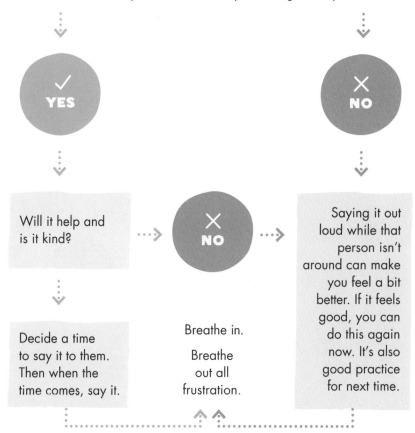

YES

NO

Will it help and is it kind?

NO

Saying it out loud while that person isn't around can make you feel a bit better. If it feels good, you can do this again now. It's also good practice for next time.

Decide a time to say it to them. Then when the time comes, say it.

Breathe in.

Breathe out all frustration.

Are you having a tricky time **MAKING NEW FRIENDS**?

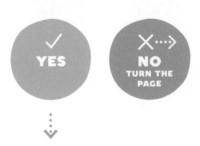

YES

NO
TURN THE PAGE

Let's figure out what's getting in the way of making new friends.

Would some more confidence help?	Are you unsure where some nice kids might be?	Not sure how to say hello?	Don't know what to say after hello?

| Stand up nice and tall and put your hands on your hips like Wonder Woman or Superman. Puff out your chest and look up to the sky.

Say out loud, "I love being me. Other kids will enjoy being friends with me." | Think about your favorite hobbies, such as playing soccer or chess.
↓
Find out where other kids are playing these games and go join in.
↓
When you find someone you like being around, ask them if they'd like to hang out with you on another day. | Turn the page → | Have a question ready about something you're interested in.

For example, "I play soccer on the weekend. What's your favorite sport?" or "I love dogs. What's your favorite animal?" |

Not sure **WHAT TO SAY** when you meet someone?

The more you say hello to new people,
the easier it gets.

Let's practice with whomever
you're sitting with right now.
Pretend you don't know them.

Stand up straight.

Walk over to them.

Smile.

Say hello.

Ask a question. For example,
"What did you do on the weekend?"

Wait for them to answer.

In real life, this is when you would keep
on chatting, asking each other questions
and answering them back and forth.

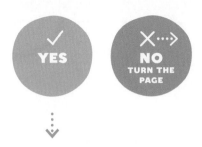

Let's switch out some of these pesky worries by swapping the nervous thoughts for confident ones.

Say out loud, "Even though I might look silly doing

_____,

[insert thing above]

I'm still going to give it a try. And even if it doesn't work out, I will still be okay."

Breathe in deeply. Breathe out all the nervous feelings.

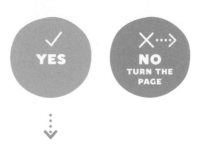

Notice what embarrassment feels like
in your body. Maybe your face is red
or your hands are sweaty.

Pretend it's two weeks from now. You
are looking back on the thing that is
embarrassing you today. Are you okay?
What have you learned?

Great job. Now, say this out loud: "I like
myself exactly as I am. I'm always doing
my best and it's okay to feel embarrassed."

Breathe in deeply. Breathe out
all embarrassment.

*NOTE TO PARENTS: *Embarrassment is the brain's reaction to
thinking we are being perceived in a way we don't like or
feeling unacceptable in some way. It can be accompanied
by blushing, sweating, stammering, and fidgeting.*

Is someone **BULLYING** or making fun of you?

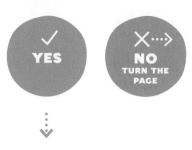

Remember, bullying is never okay.

Have you told someone, or is something being done already?

Well done for speaking up. That was very brave of you. While you wait for something to be done, say out loud, "I am brave and strong and I like myself exactly as I am."

It's time to tell someone what's happening.

As best as you can, explain what's been going on to a parent, teacher, or another grown-up.

In the meantime, keep your distance from the bully, keep being kind to yourself and your friends, and remember how wonderful you are.

Is there an upcoming **ACTIVITY** that you don't want to do?

YES **NO TURN THE PAGE**

There are always going to be things we don't want to do, but part of growing up is having to do most of them anyway.

If you feel like you haven't practiced or prepared enough, decide to do some more today.

In a friendly voice, repeat out loud, "I'm going to try my hardest and do my best to have fun."

Breathe in deeply. Breathe out all worry.

YES

X ····>
NO
TURN TO
PAGE 127

Choose which part of your life
is still on your mind:

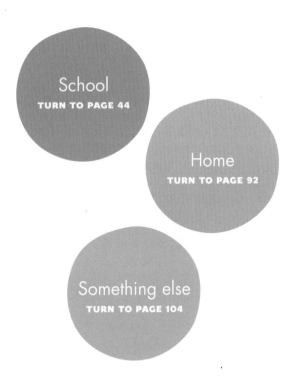

School
TURN TO PAGE 44

Home
TURN TO PAGE 92

Something else
TURN TO PAGE 104

Home

Being at home around family is usually something we enjoy, and it typically makes us feel safe. But even home can make us worry sometimes. If you are feeling any worry about your home or family . . .

TURN THE PAGE →

Are you **FEELING SCARED**
to leave your parent to go
somewhere or do something
ON YOUR OWN?

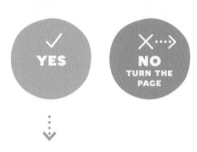

The first few times we do something on our own, it can feel scary. To help the unknown feel familiar, let's do some practicing.

With your parent, pretend you're just about to say goodbye to them. Picture where you're standing (such as in front of your school) and what you're wearing (such as your favorite outfit). Include a quick kiss, a special handshake, or a wave. Once you've finished, say out loud one thing you liked about your practice and one thing that could help you feel more comfortable.

Next time you have to say goodbye, try to follow along with your practice.

*NOTE TO PARENTS: *Separation anxiety isn't a behavioral problem to "fix"—it's an evolutionary instinct and a normal stage of childhood development. This means that even if it's tempting, it's best to avoid any urges to incentivize behavior through rewards such as a treat to stop crying. If the anxiety is particularly intense or remains for an extended period of time, it might be time to connect with a professional.*

Are you being **GRUMPY** with your family?

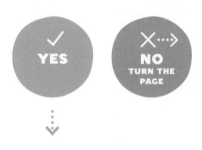

Sit up nice and straight.

Close your eyes.

Put your hands over your heart.

Say out loud, "May I be happy. May I be healthy. May I be peaceful."

Keep your eyes closed and picture your family in front of you.

Say out loud, "May they be happy. May they be healthy.
May they be peaceful."

Open your eyes. Breathe in deeply. Breathe out all grumpiness.

*NOTE TO PARENTS: *This practice of "loving-kindness" helps
to promote feelings of peace and love within. It can also
diffuse frustration and emotional intensity.*

Are you worried that something might **HAPPEN** to your **PARENTS**?

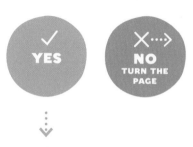

Everyone can get sick or injured at some point, and it can be a scary thing to realize it might happen to your parents. Say out loud what you are frightened might happen. Is it likely this will happen?

YES

Talk to your parents about your worries and ask how you might help them if the thing does happen.

Breathe in. Breathe out all worry.

NO

Remember that even though scary things might happen in the world, it's nice to know this one isn't very common.

Breathe in. Breathe out all worry.

Now, it's time to do something fun. You could dance to some music, draw a picture, kick a ball around, or something else.

*NOTE TO PARENTS: *While these fears are real, after they've been talked through, distraction is key to ensure that the worry doesn't develop further.*

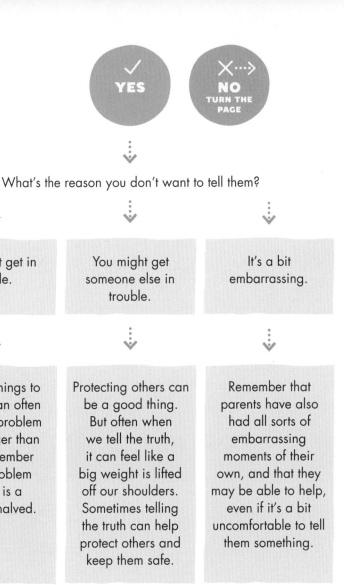

YES ✓

NO ✗ ····> TURN THE PAGE

What's the reason you don't want to tell them?

| You might get in trouble. | You might get someone else in trouble. | It's a bit embarrassing. |

| Keeping things to yourself can often make the problem seem bigger than it is. Remember that a problem shared is a problem halved. | Protecting others can be a good thing. But often when we tell the truth, it can feel like a big weight is lifted off our shoulders. Sometimes telling the truth can help protect others and keep them safe. | Remember that parents have also had all sorts of embarrassing moments of their own, and that they may be able to help, even if it's a bit uncomfortable to tell them something. |

Decide whether you would like to tell your parents now.
If it's a yes, go and tell them now or sometime today.

Are you still feeling **WORRIED** about something?

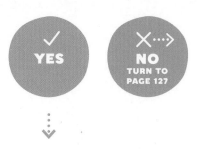

YES

NO
TURN TO
PAGE 127

Choose which part of your life is
still on your mind:

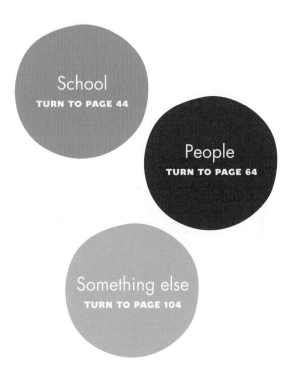

School
TURN TO PAGE 44

People
TURN TO PAGE 64

Something else
TURN TO PAGE 104

Something else

Some days, we know exactly what is worrying us, and other days, not so much. Either way . . .

TURN THE PAGE →

Big changes can feel both scary and exciting.

Fill in the blanks in the sentence below.

"Even though this big change feels

_____,

[insert tricky emotions above]

one of the good things to come from it might be

_____ .

[insert good thing above]

For the rest of the day, I'm going to choose
to think about this good thing."

Breathe in. Breathe out all worry.

Do you feel so **SAD** or **WORRIED** that your **HEART** hurts?

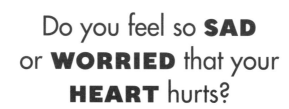

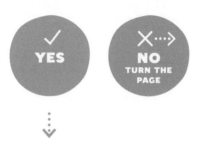

Ouch. To better understand how you're feeling, let's get drawing.

Get out a piece of paper.

Draw a picture of how your heart feels and what is happening inside of it.

Now that you can see your heart in front of you, say out loud what you think might help it feel better. For example, it could be a hug or going outside for some fresh air.

If possible, go and do that thing.

*NOTE TO PARENTS: *Kids who are particularly emotionally sensitive often have extra awareness when it comes to other people's feelings and the emotional temperature of situations. Remember that this can be a helpful quality that, when nurtured, can allow kids to strengthen their intuition and creativity. Keep an eye out for any overstimulation that may exacerbate the more difficult parts of their sensitivity.*

EXTRA NOTE: *This might also be a nice time to do the Anytime Meditation Script on page 140.*

Have you seen something on **TV**, in a **BOOK**, or on the **INTERNET** that has made you worried or scared?

Sometimes scary things happen, and it's normal
to feel worried.

Say out loud what the scary thing is and how it's worried you.

Talk it through with a grown-up and ask any
questions you've got.

Breathe in deeply. Breathe out all worry.

*NOTE TO PARENTS: *If relevant, you could do the following:*
*· On a map, show where the event happened to demonstrate
the big distance if it took place far away.*
· Explain that replays on TV aren't the same event happening again.
· Talk about how rarely these events occur.
· Give facts that help debunk fears.
*· Talk about who is helping in the situation, such as firefighters,
police, or nurses.*
· Where possible, limit media exposure to frightening topics.

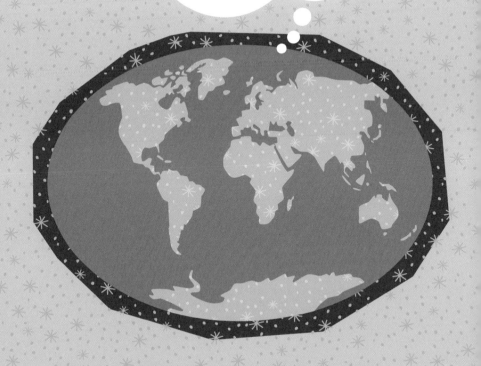

Big events can be scary for people of all ages.

Ask a grown-up any questions you've got about it.

Now, let's find some happy things going on in the world.

With your grown-up, list two or more good things happening in the world.

BONUS: Create a scrapbook of good things happening in the world.

Does it feel like you look **DIFFERENT** from others?

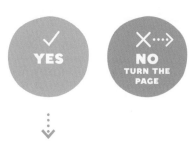

Did you know that every single body in the world is different? Identical twins even have differences! Even though it might be hard feeling like you look different, it's our differences that make us who we are.

List three amazing things your body can do.
Here are some ideas to get you started:

Run fast
Use a jump rope
Catch a ball
See clearly
Hear when people speak
Smell chocolate
Climb a ladder
Make silly faces

Are you struggling to fall **ASLEEP**?

Sometimes our minds get very busy right before bedtime.
One of the reasons for this is that we may not have had enough
quiet time during the day. This means that when we finally
slow down, our brain bubbles over with too many thoughts.

To help find some calm, you can choose from one of these things to do:

Breathe.
Lie down in your
bed and take
three big, deep,
and slow breaths
in and out.

Read.
Choose one story
to read from your
bookshelf.

Meditate.
Ask a parent to read
out the Anytime
Meditation Script on
page 140 while you
lie down in bed with
your eyes closed.

*NOTE TO PARENTS: Remember, people of all ages have trouble falling
asleep. If difficulty falling asleep is a common occurrence in your home, you
might like to consider how well your sleep hygiene (what happens in the
hours leading up to bedtime) is going. To improve it, consider these tips for
the hours before bed: no screens, caffeine (remembering that chocolate has
caffeine in it), or scary shows and stories; minimal sugar; dimmed lights;
and reading or playing calm music.*

Say out loud what the scariest thing about the dark is for you.

Think of a way you could prove that worry to be untrue.

If that idea is possible right now, carry out your plan with a parent or another grown-up.

For example, the scariest thing about the dark might be worry that something is lurking in the shadows. An idea to prove that this isn't true might be to shine a flashlight at the shadow and check that there's nothing there.

DID YOU KNOW?

A very long time ago, when our ancestors lived in nature and shared the land with possible enemies and large animals, they learned to be cautious of the dark. This fear was helpful because it kept kids and babies from wandering away in the middle of the night and made sure everyone was safe. Now that we live in houses, that risk is something we no longer have to worry about.

Are you
feeling
AFRAID
that there
is a **GHOST**
in the room?

Repeat this out loud:
"I ask for all energy that is not mine to
please leave this room/house immediately.
Please leave peacefully and do not return.
I wish you well on your journey."

Picture that energy leaving.

Breathe in. Breathe out all feelings
of being scared.

*NOTE TO PARENTS: *The feeling of some other energy in the room can
be a very scary experience, particularly for kids. Whether their concerns
seem true or not, giving kids a voice in identifying what they feel
and helping them to do something about it is very empowering.*

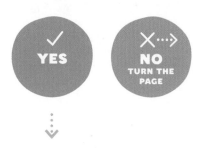

Do you feel comfortable saying your problem out loud?

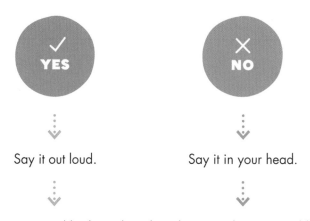

Say it out loud.   Say it in your head.

If a very wise owl had an idea about how to solve your problem,
what do you think it might say?

Say out loud what first step you could take.

Do that first step.

Are you finding
it **HARD** to
FIGURE OUT
what's making you
feel worried?

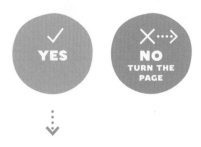

Tap on the "karate chop" point on your hand.

.... Karate chop point

While you're tapping, say out loud three times, "Even though I don't know exactly what's making me feel worried, I know I'm still a good kid."

While continuing to tap your hand, say out loud, "Even though there might still be things on my mind, I'm really proud of everything I've just worked through."

Stop tapping. Breathe in and breathe out.

NOTE TO PARENTS: *This activity works best when you do it at the same time as your child. It's recommended that you break up the statements into chunks that your child repeats after you. This practice is based on Emotional Freedom Techniques.*

PART FOUR

Checking in again

Let's check in with how
you're feeling now.

Right now,
WHICH FACE
describes how
you are
FEELING?

SAD · ANGRY · SILLY · HAPPY

FRUSTRATED · SHY · SCARED · EXCITED

WORRIED · LONELY · LEFT OUT · OVERWHELMED

TIRED · SICK · EMBARRASSED · CALM

*NOTE TO PARENTS: *Whether these feelings have shifted or stayed the same, remember that talking through them is always a good thing. Notice what did and didn't bring relief to your child. This will help inform your day-to-day emotional management and interactions.*

On a scale
from 1 to 10, how
STRONG are those
FEELINGS?

1 2 3

4 5 6 7

8 9 10

Did going through this book bring you some calm?

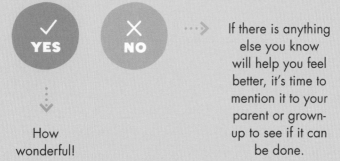

YES

How wonderful!

NO ····▷ If there is anything else you know will help you feel better, it's time to mention it to your parent or grown-up to see if it can be done.

Feeling
PROUD
of today's
EFFORTS!

Well done for working your way
through all—or a little bit—of this book.
It takes lots of courage to talk about our
feelings, and you have done exactly that.

●

Whenever you feel worried,
you can always read this book.

●

It's time to take a big breath in.
And a big breath out.

●

REMEMBER:
You have done a great job today.
You are very loved.
You are a great kid.

FOR PARENTS & CAREGIVERS

HELPFUL

TIPS

Model upbeat, confident thinking.

Remember that you don't need to be perfect to help your child.

Take care of your own emotional well-being.

Balance both learning and play.

Give your child the space to make mistakes by not completing their homework on their behalf.

Do your best to not get emotionally swept up in your child's feelings.

Remember that all feelings are acceptable, but all behavior is not. Do your best to manage unhelpful behaviors while upholding family boundaries.

Focus on your child's efforts, not their outcomes.

When appropriate, share your own examples of making errors or times when you've felt nervous and how you got through them.

Aim to have a light and centered approach when talking about feelings.

If your child's anxiety continues, or if it could be the result of a traumatic experience, reach out for professional help.

CALMING
rituals for your child

To maintain momentum in between readings
of this book, here are some extra activities
you may like to try out with your child.

VISUALIZATION
During bath or
shower time, suggest
that your child visualize
all their worries washing
off and going down
the drain.

GRATITUDE
Before bed or at
dinnertime, have
everyone in your family
say three things they are
grateful for or enjoyed
during their day.

GROUNDING

To help ground your child's energy, spend as much time as possible outside connecting with nature. This could include playing in parks, hiking, spending time at the beach, or just having bare feet in your backyard.

MEDITATION

Instilling a meditation practice from a young age is a wonderful gift to your child. You might like to try some kids' meditations from an app or online, or read out the one on page 140. As a guide, kids can generally meditate for the number of minutes corresponding with their age—that is, a seven-year-old could work up to meditating for seven minutes.

EXERCISE

Make sure movement is part of your child's day every day. It doesn't matter if it's organized sports, playing in the nearest park, or walking the dog— anything helps!

AFFIRMATIONS

Affirmations are a simple and effective way to help calm busy minds. They are positive statements that begin to feel and become true when repeated. You might like to read these out each morning with your child.

I am a good kid.

Trying my best is a great place to start.

I am safe.

I choose to feel peaceful.

I allow myself to have fun.

It's safe for me to breathe deeply.

My brain is amazing.

Interruptions are okay.

Mistakes help me learn.

I relax with every breath I take.

I am calm and comfortable.

The Anytime **MEDITATION** Script

Meditation is an amazing tool for calming busy minds and hearts. It can give both kids and adults a sense of safety and peace that strengthens everyday resilience and happiness. Use this script whenever your child needs it and enjoy the calm it brings you too. It is recommended that you read this out calmly, slowly, and with regular pauses to allow plenty of time for the visual components to be formed. It should take around three to five minutes.

To begin, have your child gently lie or sit down
with their eyes closed. Read out the following:

*As you settle in, start by taking a big breath in through your
nose, and now, release that big breath out through your mouth.
I want you now to imagine high up in the sky above us the great,
big sun. Notice what shape the sun is and what colors it is made up
of. Now, see a very large beam of sunshine coming down from the
sun all the way to your forehead. Feel the warmth of that sunbeam
as it dances on your face. Now, let the warmth of the sunshine start
to fill up the whole of your head, helping it feel warm and cozy.
Watch as the warmth starts to move down your neck, your arms,
and your chest. Notice how the warmth is now filling up your belly,
your legs, and all the way down to your feet. Feel that
sunshine going into each toe.*

*I want you now to look into your body and notice if there are
any worries sitting inside. If you notice one or maybe even more,
know that you are safe. Now, see the string of a balloon tying
itself to each of the worries. Notice what color the balloons are and
the shapes of the balloons. Now, one by one, let each balloon
float up into the sky, taking your worries with it. As the worry leaves
your body, notice a feeling of lightness sweep through you.*

*Whenever you are ready, you can wiggle your toes.
Wiggle your fingers. Now, gently blink your eyes back open.*

Acknowledgments

•

Creating books that make an impact is just one of the reasons I adore working with the teams at Murdoch Books and The Experiment. The privilege of sharing this book with North American families is something I am deeply grateful for. Thank you to The Experiment for choosing to nurture the minds and hearts of children through this book. Special shout-outs to Hannah Matuszak, Jennifer Hergenroeder, Jane Morrow, Virginia Birch, Britta Martins-Simon, Kristy Allen, Sue Bobbermein, Ariana Klepac, Michelle Mackintosh, and Lou Johnson—you are all game changers, and you do it with heart, intellect, and grace.

In my experience, books are a culmination of experience, information, heart, and the people who surround the author. For helping me to bring this book to life, a special thank-you goes to all the children and inner children I've taught and coached—you remind me how to see the bright side of life, and for that I'm grateful. To Taylan, Oakley, Kyla, Levi, Sydney, and Madison, it's a joy to be a part of your family. Thank you for continuing to teach me how to play. To Ivan, thank you for always being in my corner and for bringing our very own heart-filled human into the world with me.

The biggest honor of my life has been becoming a mom to our Ruby. As you grow and learn, my wish is that you enjoy the full breadth of the world in all its complexity and that you treat your mind, body, and spirit with kindness and awe. Thank you for choosing me to be your mom. You have brought me a calm and happiness that I have never before experienced.

P.S. For those who love the world's kids, a big thank-you for helping our next generation bolster their confidence, groundedness, and self-respect. To the parents, teachers, childcare workers, psychologists, counselors, grandparents, godparents, neighbors, health-care workers, and playgroup leaders—by investing part of your energy into the kids of the world, you're making the earth a kinder, more productive, happier, better place. Thank you.

Resources

•

For emergency support, please contact a helpline:

Your Life Your Voice | 1.800.448.3000 | yourlifeyourvoice.org

Kids Help Phone | 1.800.668.6868 | kidshelpphone.ca

Parents looking for extra help supporting their kid can use these resources:

American Academy of Child & Adolescent Psychiatry | aacap.org

Child Mind Institute | childmind.org

National Alliance on Mental Illness | nami.org

National Institute of Mental Health | nimh.nih.gov

The Experiment, LLC | 220 East 23rd Street, Suite 600 | New York, NY 10010-4658
theexperimentpublishing.com

THE EXPERIMENT and its colophon are registered trademarks of The Experiment, LLC. Many of the designations used by manufacturers and sellers to distinguish their products are claimed as trademarks. Where those designations appear in this book and The Experiment was aware of a trademark claim, the designations have been capitalized.

The Experiment's books are available at special discounts when purchased in bulk for premiums and sales promotions as well as for fundraising or educational use. For details, contact us at info@theexperimentpublishing.com.

Library of Congress Cataloging-in-Publication Data

Names: Kirkness, Tammi, author.
Title: Why do I feel so worried? : a kid's guide to coping with big
    Emotions—follow the arrows from anxiety to calm / Tammi Kirkness.
Description: New York : The Experiment, 2022. | Audience: Ages 7-12 |
    Audience: Grades 4-6
Identifiers: LCCN 2021046143 (print) | LCCN 2021046144 (ebook) | ISBN
    9781615198733 (paperback) | ISBN 9781615198894 (ebook)
Subjects: LCSH: Anxiety–Juvenile literature. | Calmness–Juvenile
    literature. | Emotions–Juvenile literature.
Classification: LCC BF575.A6 K576 2022 (print) | LCC BF575.A6 (ebook) |
    DDC 152.4/6–dc23/eng/20211106
LC record available at https://lccn.loc.gov/2021046143
LC ebook record available at https://lccn.loc.gov/2021046144

ISBN 978-1-61519-873-3
Ebook ISBN 978-1-61519-889-4

Cover design by Beth Bugler
Illustrations and text design by Murdoch Books

Manufactured in China

First printing March 2022
10 9 8 7 6 5 4 3 2